My Mighty Silent Me

A Collection of Poems

Written By
Susan McMachan

And Illustrated By
**Terri Ann Morgan,
Peter Rabasco,
Clarissa Eck,
Melissa Skiadas,
&
Stephanie Skiadas**

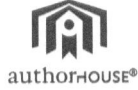
authorHOUSE®

AuthorHouse™
1663 Liberty Drive, Suite 200
Bloomington, IN 47403
www.authorhouse.com
Phone: 1-800-839-8640

First published by AuthorHouse 3/15/2008

ISBN: 978-1-4343-5818-9 (sc)

Printed in the United States of America
Bloomington, Indiana

This book is printed on acid-free paper.

This book is dedicated to:
My wonderful family and dear friends.
Thank you for your unwavering
Love and support during this project.

And

A very special thank you
to Ted Braggins, and the
"Completely, ridiculously, awesome"
young artists at Arlington High.

Table of Contents

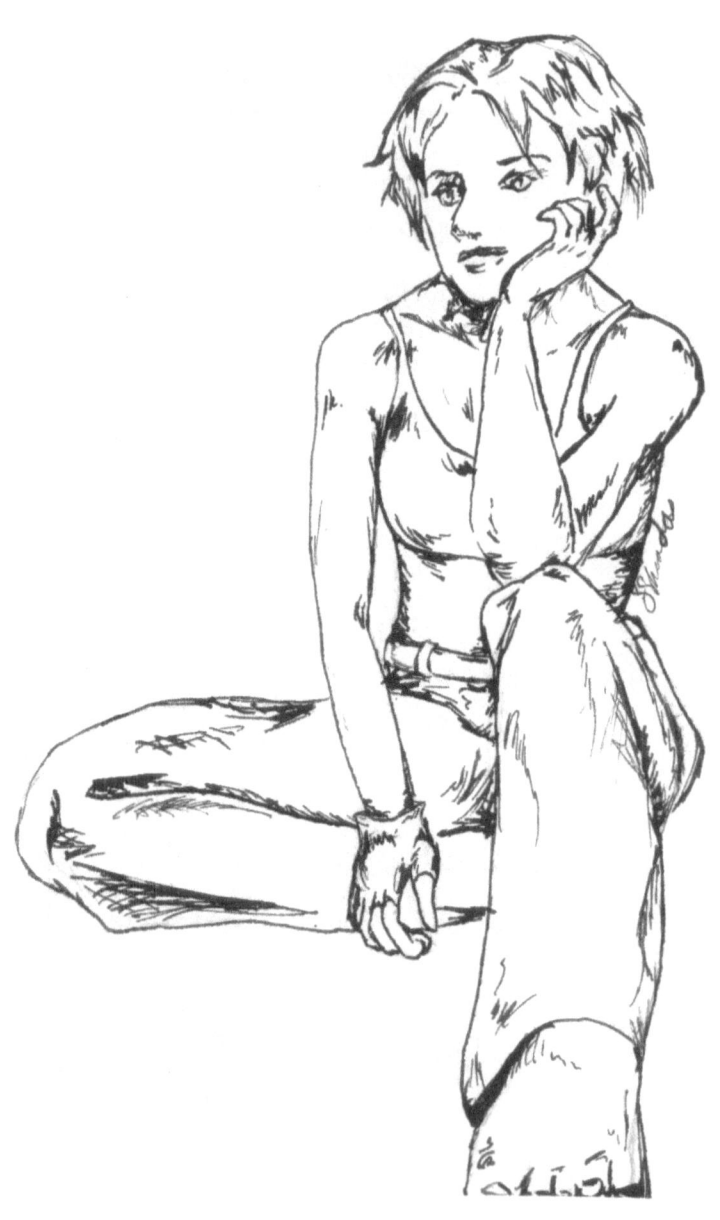

My Mighty Silent Me

If you could look inside of me,
Through my eyes, a clear blue sea,
And plunge into the depth of me,
You'd find my mighty silent me.

The guardian of all that's me,
Blushing shades of possibility
And ringlets, bright with reverie,
Adorn my mighty silent me.

A sentinel of strength is she
Who wears a crest of lion's three,
That roars with immortality,
The soul of my mighty silent me.

One lion for love's joy in me,
One speaks in fluent honesty,
The last one holds hope's destiny.
Guide wise my mighty silent me.

That steady voice that speaks to me
When I stumble blind and cannot see,
She leads me to the core of me,
Rest well in my mighty silent me.

And respite safe in her certainty,
She reaffirms my faith in me,
And face to face, with me to me,
Reawakens my mighty silent me

Boldly gaze, through the eyes you see,
See all that went into making me,
And see revealed abundantly.
Peace reigns my mighty silent me.

What matters how the world sees me
Or storms at my periphery,
It cannot change my clear blue sea
Or silence my mighty silent me.

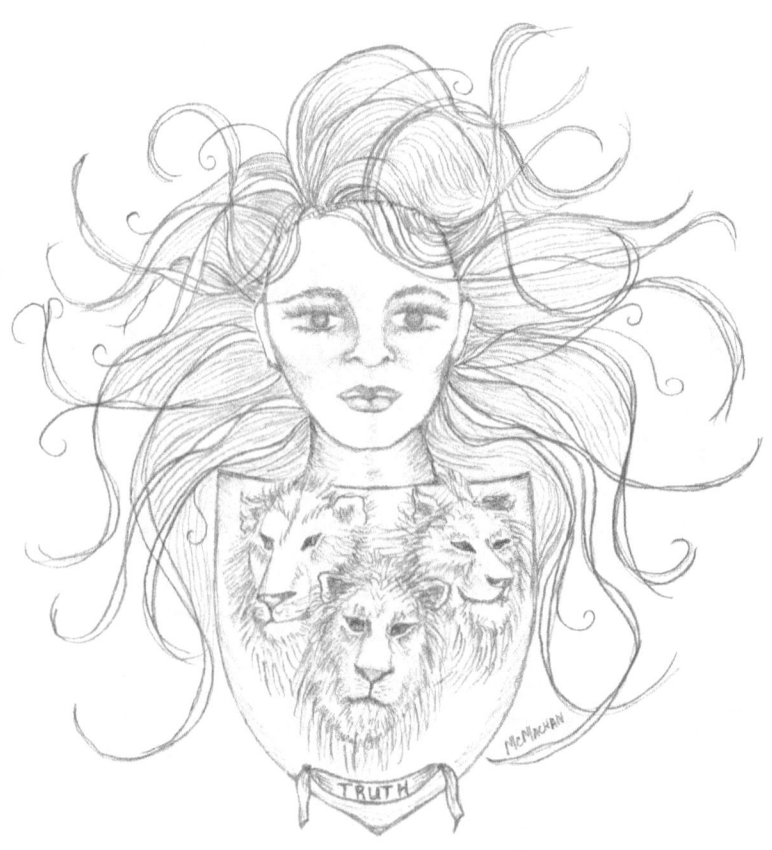

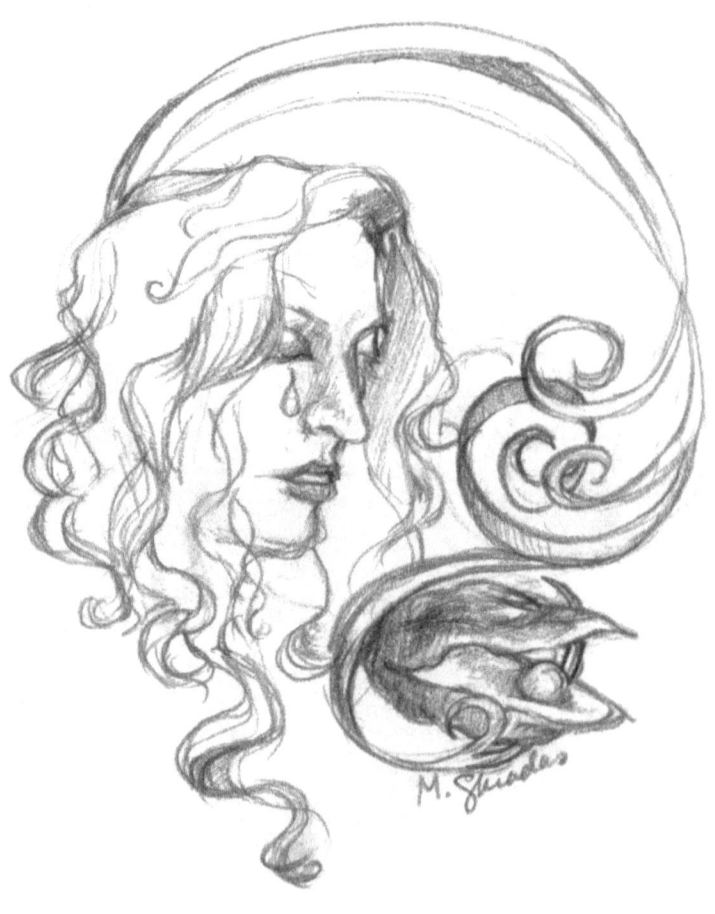

The Oyster's Sorrow

Sorrow has the Oyster,
A random speck of sand,
Flowed ebb and tide
To end it's ride,
In Oyster's mouth did land.

It soon became a sorrow.
Oyster layered it with pearl,
And it spent its life
In sacrifice
To work a miracle

The Oyster died for sorrow.
Its mouth lay gaping wide,
So I took my hand
And plucked the sand
That was buried deep inside

I amazed upon this sorrow,
As tears rained down my face.
It gleamed with light,
My breath took flight,
The sand had turned to grace.

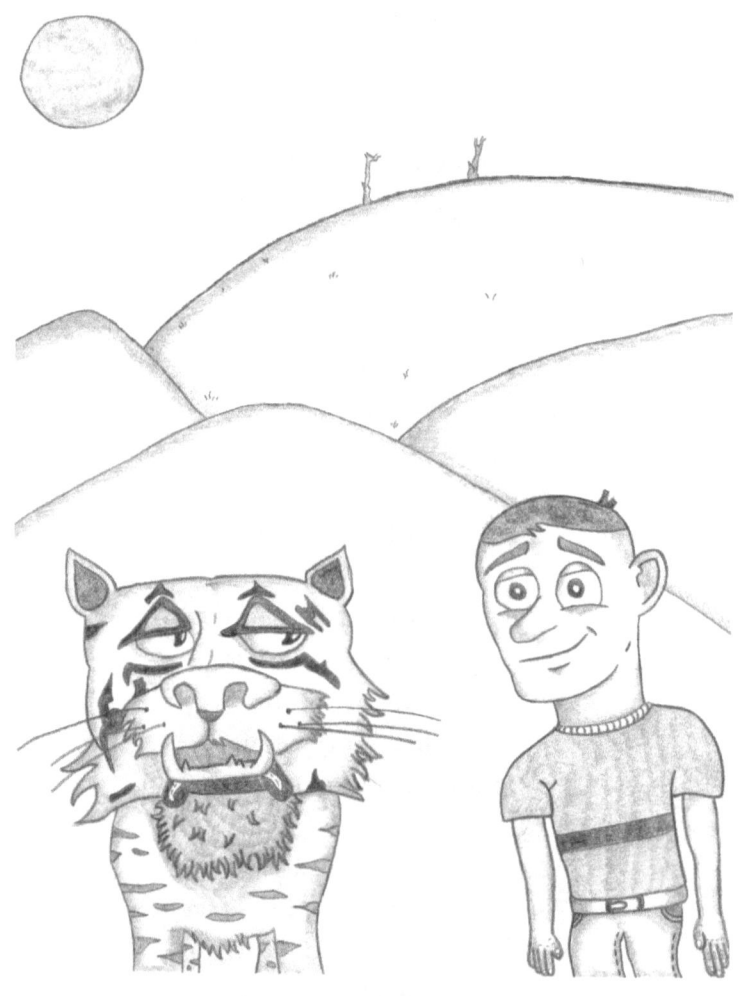

The Tiger's Toe and Miney Mo

Eeny Meeny Miney Mo,
Caught a tiger by the toe.
He didn't holler, he growled instead,
Then chased him all around his bed.

Eeny cried, "I've let you go,
Why do you still chase me so?"
Tiger said, "Well when we meet,
You're always pulling at my feet!"

"And boy, my toe is getting sore,
So I won't let you pull it more.
If you can't stop and be my friend,
I might just eat you in the end!"

Eeny Meeny scratched his head
And thought about what Tiger said.
Then Eeny said, "I didn't know
That catching you would hurt your toe."

"I only want to be your friend
And I won't pull your toe again."
Tiger said, "That would be fine,
My good friend, Eeny Meeny mine."

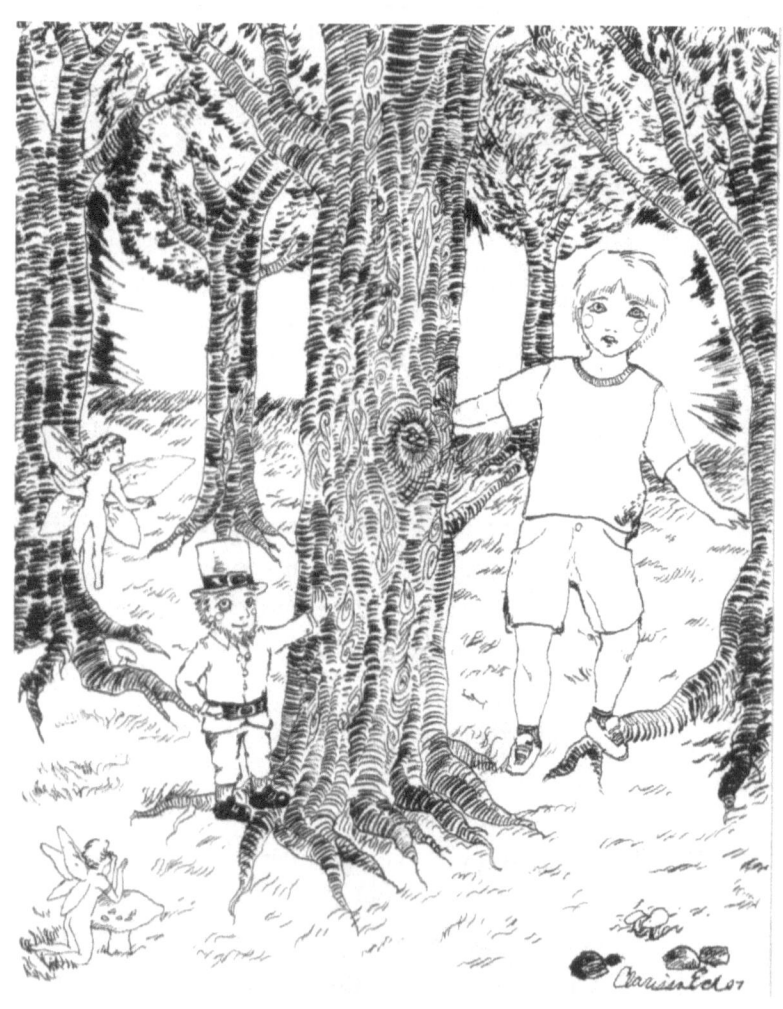

The Forest of the Leprechauns

A magic place where I have gone,
The forest of the Leprechauns,
Holds secret, hidden pots of gold
In trees with little, ancient holds.

There gleaming strands of platinum sun
All lace together, then come undone
In wispy, waves on the forest floor.
Great patterns from the canopy pour.

And hop scotch fairies, on spots of light,
Who disappear in shadowy flight,
Then giggle when they reappear,
And flutter here and there and near.

The Leprechauns play "Hide and Seek."
They sneak around the trees and peek,
And laugh until they're falling down,
And wrestle on the soft, green ground.

They stash away small pots of gold.
At least that's how this story's told,
And then forget their hiding places
While rumbling round and running races.

And though they're old in ancient years,
They've never left their childhood here.
So play they must, and hide and seek,
And find their gold, then lose its keep.

But they know when their gold is gone,
When it's taken by no Leprechaun.
When it's stolen from their game instead,
Then darker days are just ahead.

Without their gold they have no game.
We'd know them by another name,
Like Dwarves or Trolls, or maybe Elves.
Leprechauns wouldn't be themselves.

Then the forest wouldn't be the same
And it would have to change its name.
For if hiding places weren't needed
The trees would never be reseeded.

So the trees would leave the forest too.
Then what would all the fairies do?
If they can't hop scotch spots of light
They'll hurry out in hurried flight.

And there would be no "Hide and Seek,"
Nor trees to sneak around and peek.
The ancient years would catch them then,
And turn the Leprechauns to men.

Then the Leprechauns would surely scare
The forest creatures everywhere.
And they would have to leave, I fear,
Leave behind their childhood here.

So, if ever you should chance to come
Where gleaming strands of platinum sun
Wave wispy on the forest floor,
And fairies dance and dart and soar,

And if you should find small pots of gold
In trees with ancient, secret holds,
Leave the gold and walk away.
Let Leprechauns play and play and play.

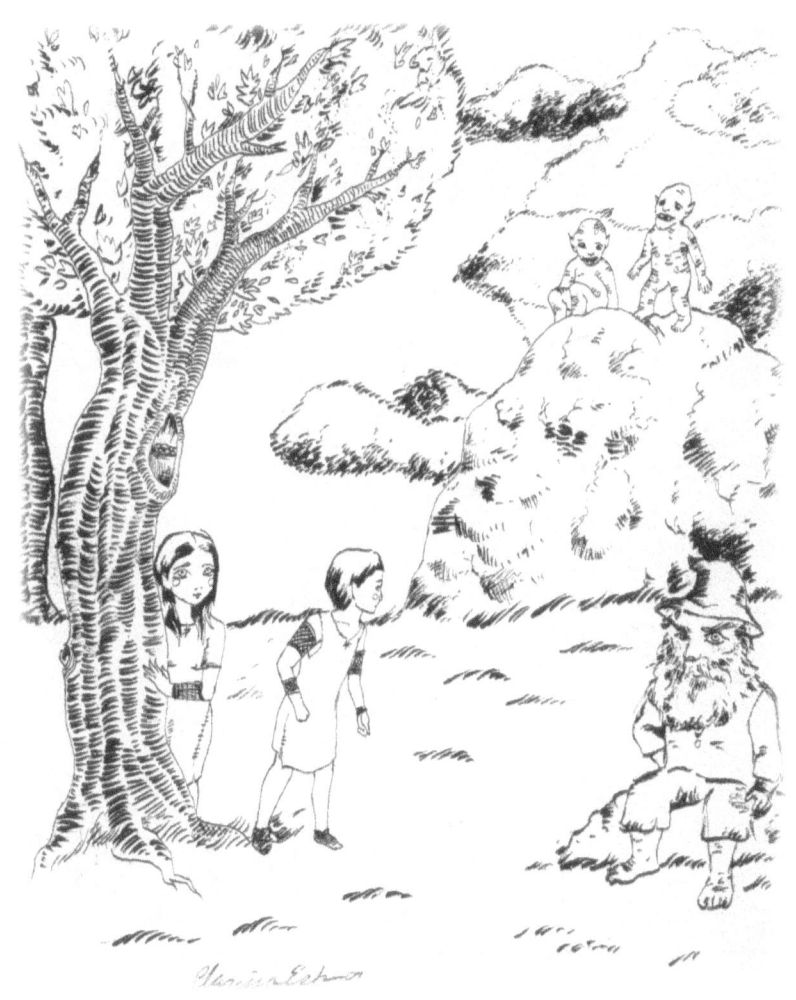

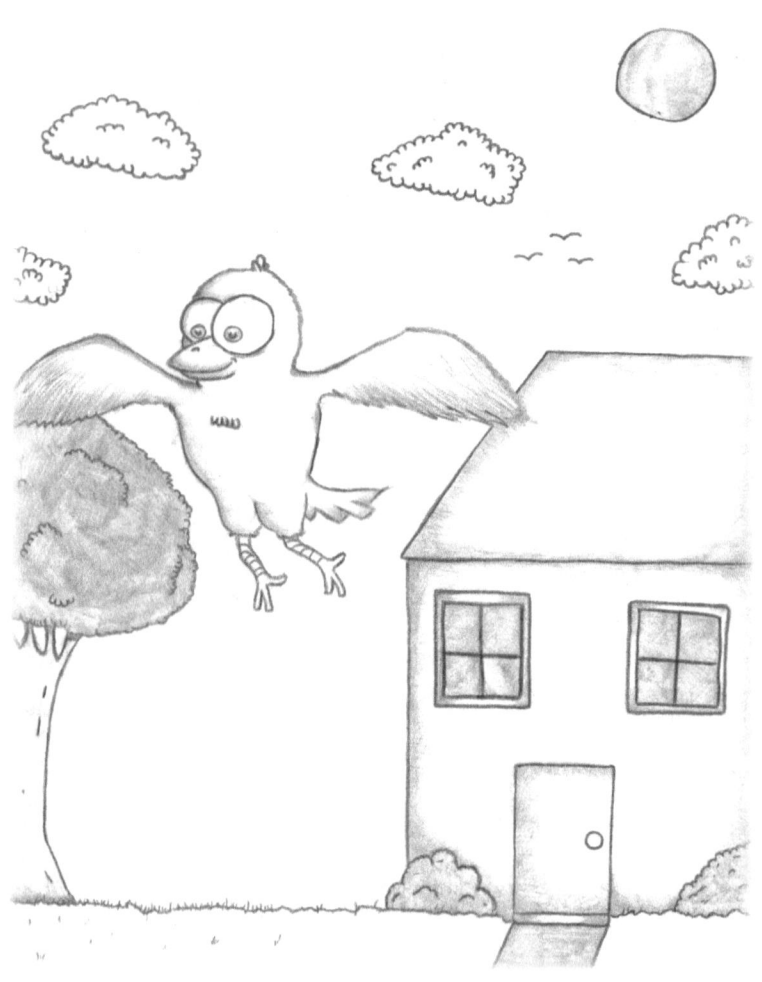

Twitter Tweeter

Twitter Tweeter jumps away,
He wants to learn to fly today.

Pitter Patter tiny feet,
He hops along the window seat.

Teeter Totter on the ledge,
He thinks that he can make the hedge.

Flitter Flutter wings so high,
To fly the way the others fly.

Spitter Sputter to the chair,
He only made it half way there.

Chitter Chatter, takes a rest,
And wonders why he flew the nest!

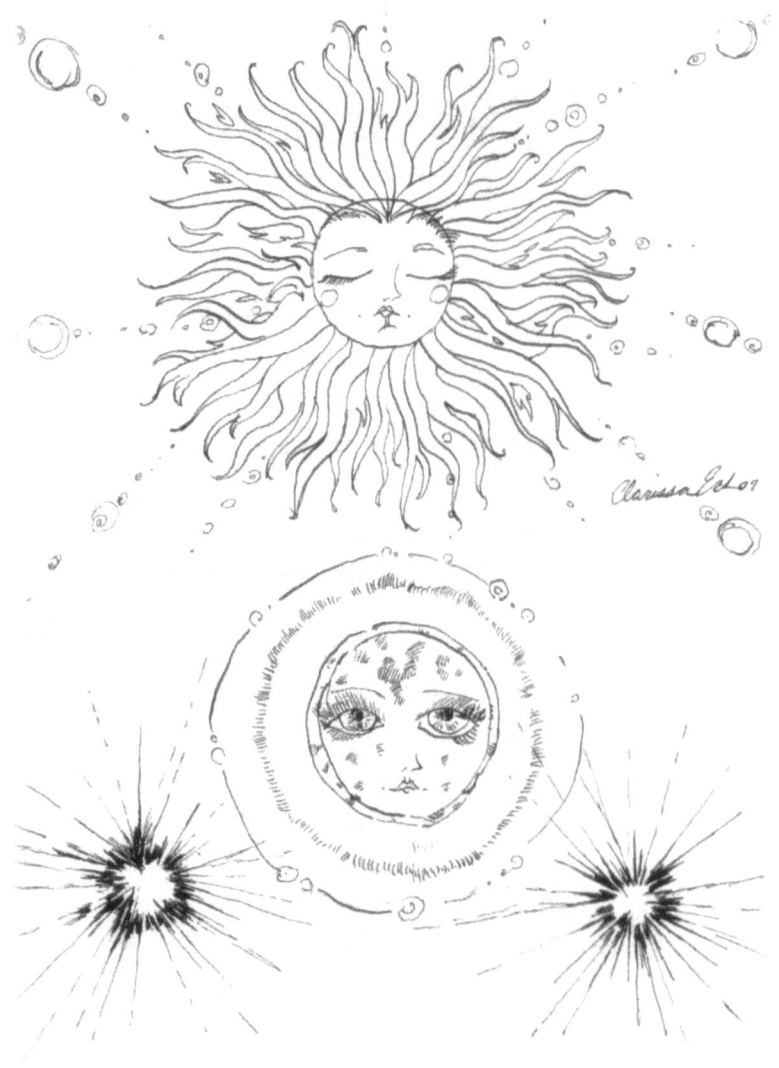

The Race between
the Moon and Sun

"Ready or not, for here I come!"
Cried the Moon and chased the Sun.
"Stick em' up and hold em' high,
Or I might Shoot You from the Sky!"

The Sun called back, "Okay, I'll flee,
Let's see if you keep up with me!"
An Ancient Chase had just begun,
The Race between the Moon and Sun.

The Sun rose up into the sky,
"Did you not know that I could fly?"
The Moon just laughed and rose up too,
"Oh, I can do what you can do."

The Sun plumped up a cloud and sat,
"Alright, you fly. I'll give you that.
But tell me, can you warm the breeze,
Or grow the flowers, plants and trees?"

The Moon said, "Sun, wake up your Eyes!
It's me that makes the oceans rise,
And me who is the beacon light
While you sleep on the job at night."

The Sun cried, "Moon, you must be high!
I light your face that lights the sky!"
"Well, ready or not," the Moon replied,
"For you there is no place to hide!"

The Sun flew down and made away.
He found himself a brand new day
And hung out there in skies so blue
Until the Moon came into view.

And still they chase from east to west
And put their talents to the test.
The Sun flies with the daylight's stride,
The Moon surfs on the midnight tide.

Though neither one will win, you see,
The longest chase in history.
No Sun nor Moon has ever won
The Race between the Moon and Sun.

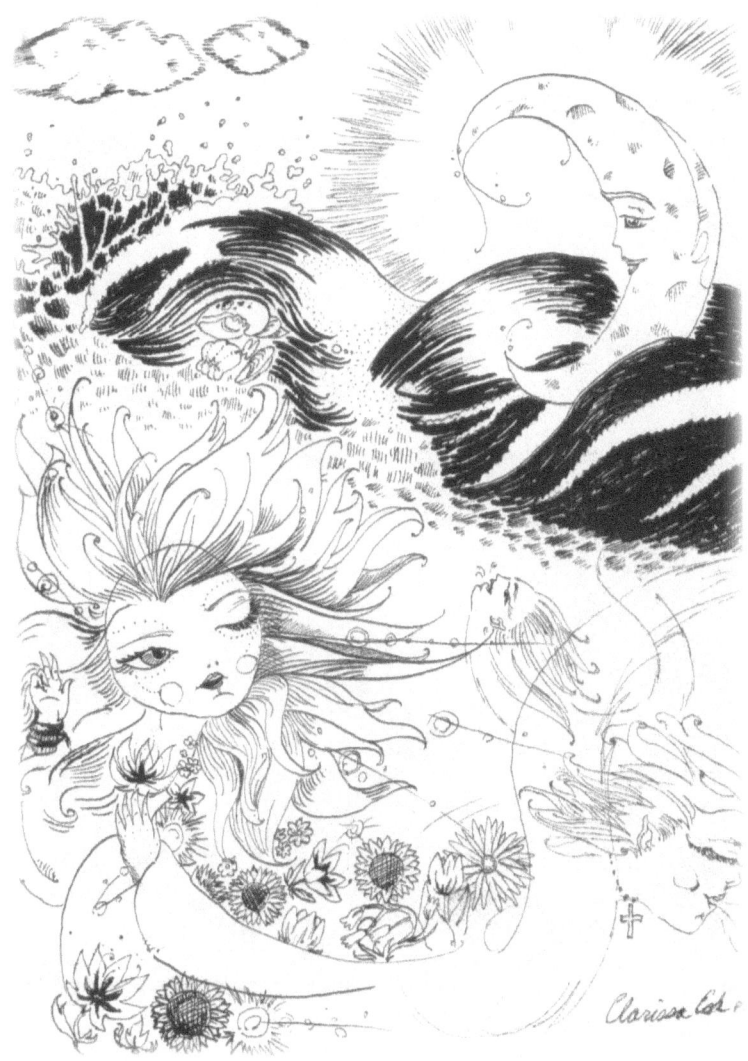

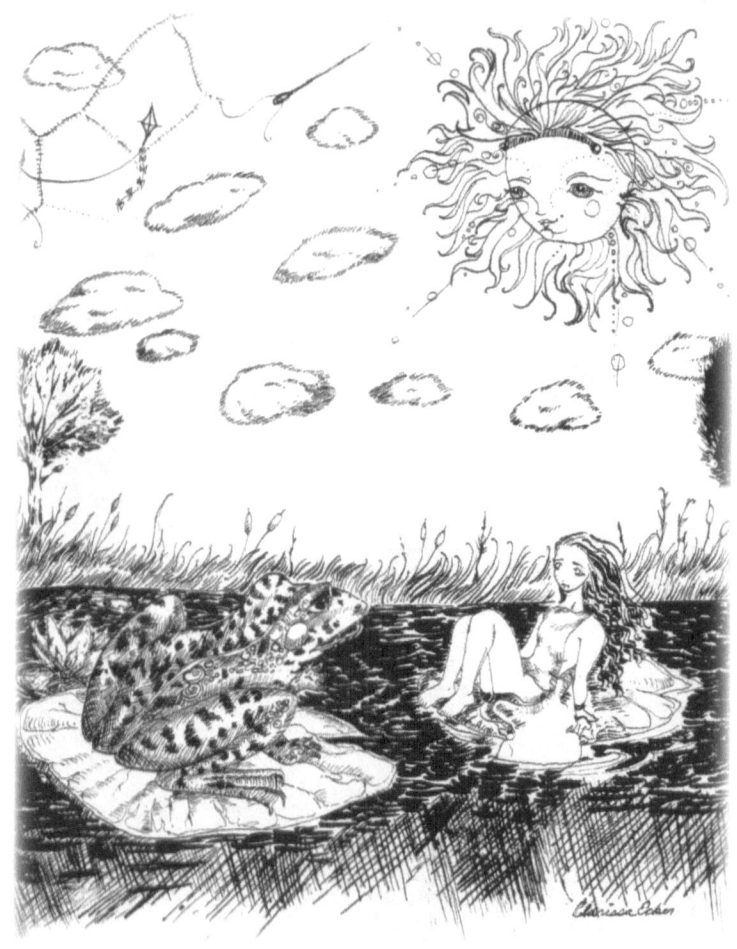

Mr. Frog and I

I sat upon a lily pad
And floated gently by,
Along with my companion,
Just Mr. Frog and I.
We sailed on rippling waters,
Past a forestry of reeds
And reminisced of days gone by
And all our worldly deeds.

Then Mr. Frog confided
That he felt he'd come up short,
And he put a webbed hand
To my lips to quiet my retort.
"They say I am a bully,
and they say it with good reason,
For I was not this kindly frog
When I was in my season."

But I said, "You're mistaken
And I know you can't be serious!
I'm sure you've caught a fever sir,
And therefore are delirious."
"I was a double agent," he pressed,
"A truly cunning spy,
And I snatched the life from many
As they floated gently by."

"Oh Frog," I cried, "what words have I
As we sail upon this leaf?
Not one of us is innocent
In causing others grief."
"I was a fearsome bullfrog," he said,

"Content to play my part,
And the only thing that I have feared
Is this changing of my heart."

"But Frog," I said, "You're not alone
In the sadness that you feel.
So many, did I float right by,
That I had the chance to heal."
Said Frog, "The Great Creator
Has put me to a test,
And the change that's happened to my heart
Is aching in my chest.

I said, "If you are sorry
For the mean things that you've done,
Then misery will leave your heart
And the peace you seek will come.
And then you'll be as happy
As a frog could ever be,
As you sail on rippling waters,
On a lily pad with me."

So there, we prayed together
For the saving of his soul,
And I asked the Great Creator
That he make my dear friend whole.
Then Mr. Frog grew giant wings
And leaped into the sky!
He beamed a smile down on me,
Then floated gently by.

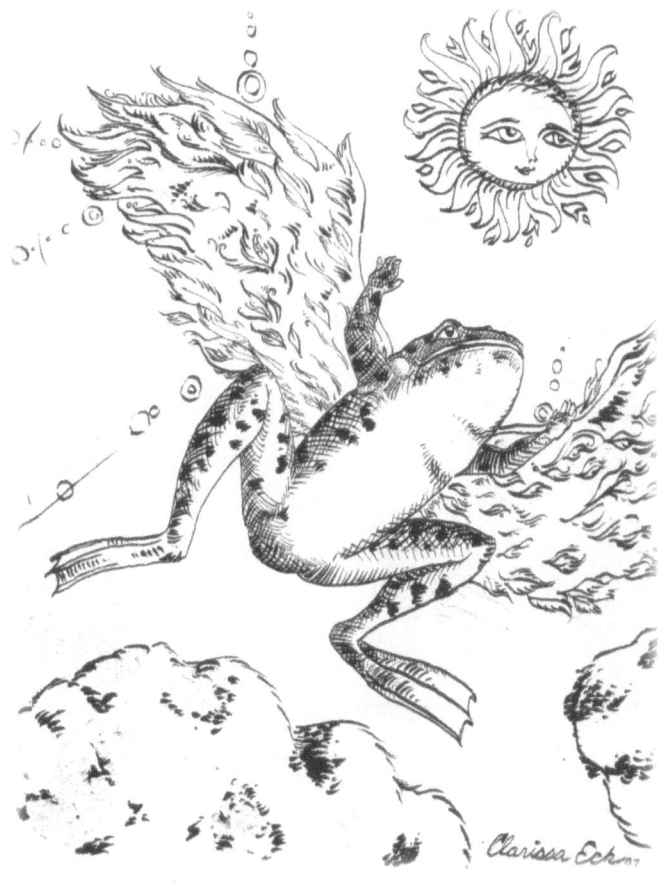

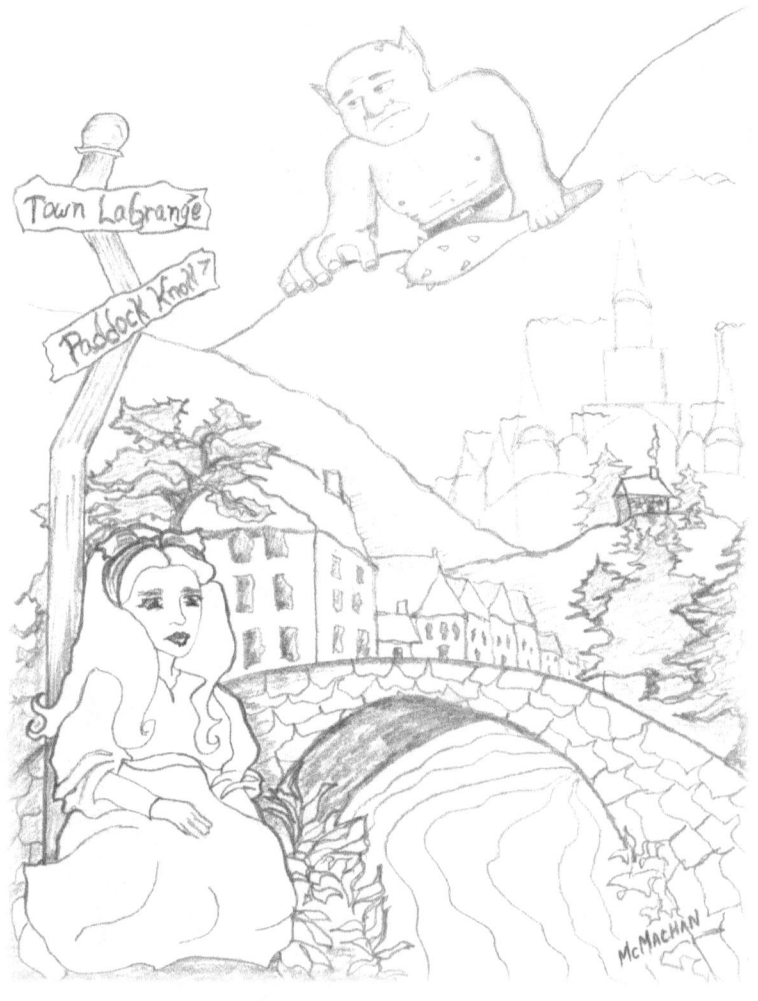

The Little Stone Cottage at Paddock Knoll

My road in life was bending strange
When it came upon the town LaGrange,
Where pastures opened wide and green,
With boulder mountains and rushing streams.
A multitude of flying things
From butterflies to feathered wings
Showered in the sweetened air,
Delighting on the flowers there
And circled round a signage pole
That showed the way to Paddock Knoll.

The miles on the road conspired
And I found that I was very tired,
When an Oak tree knelt to offer quick
A sturdy, knotted walking stick,
And pointed out the vast allotage,
A hidden hill and a small stone cottage.
My journey begged to refuge there,
Was weary of the thoroughfare,
And quiet sought my restless soul
As I trailed along to Paddock Knoll.

I nearly fell upon my knees
When I reached a glade of piney trees.
Then just beyond, I climbed the hill,
Through forget-me-nots and daffodils
And marveled that my wanderlust
Was vanishing like fairy dust.
Then cried the tiny house of stone,
"You're almost here, you're almost home."
And beautiful was the scene I stole
When first I gazed at Paddock Knoll.

No kingly palace did I embrace,
Nor stately mansion would I grace,
Or think that I could better trade
This cottage in the hilltop glade.
For through an arch of Mandeville,
It crowned the tiny hidden hill
With jewels of colored cobblestones,
Was nestled in the clear alone,
That viewed the panorama whole,
The kingdom there at Paddock Knoll.

The chimney breathed great puffs of smoke.
It cleared its stony throat and spoke,
"I've called to you for many years,
So glad I am you're finally here.
Your journey can at last retire,
The mice have made a steady fire.
The birds flew open shutters wide,
The squirrels prepared a meal inside."
Then a rabbit bowed before it's hole
Singing, "Hail the Queen of Paddock Knoll!"

My subjects were a furry sight.
I dubbed the woodchuck my First Knight,
And saw afar a paddock ring
With mighty horses soldiering,
That whinnied to the hawk and owl
And all the many feathered fowl,
"Send out the call, send up the cry,
The mistress of our Knoll's arrived!"
And I pledged my heart and grateful soul
To justly rule at Paddock Knoll.

Then the cottage grew before my eyes
To a great and truly awesome size.
And trumpets sounded in the air,
Heralding a castle fair.
Spires sprang through treetops high.
They waved huge banners in the sky.
Then all the creatures rushed to order
And the woodchuck cried, "Protect the border!"
When all at once three giant Trolls
Came thundering toward Paddock Knoll.

The Dragonflies launched their attack,
"Save the queen!" they shouted back.
And stabbed the monsters' knarly feet
In hopes that they would then retreat.
But they ran steady towards their deed.
I jumped aback my strongest steed
And signaled with a arrow shot
To send the Squirrels in chariots,
Then set the tower bells to toll
When we took the field at Paddock Knoll.

The deer charged in with antlers drawn.
Fox, wolves and rabbits filled the lawn.
The skunks raised tails up fierce and high
And let some crazy stink-bombs fly.
The Trolls succumbed to my mighty forces,
Were dragged away by my faithful horses.
So I praised the troops with celebration.
They saved the day, their queen, and nation!
Then to my castle bed I stole
And I dreamed away my Paddock Knoll.

I woke upon a mossy green,
Beside a winding, rushing stream,
And saw a sign pole bending strange
That said this was the "Town La Grange."
And "Paddock Knoll" pointed to a hill
Of forget-me-nots and daffodils,
And I knew that I was headed there,
Though how I knew, I couldn't swear.
But I'm sure I heard a small house call,
"Come home, come home to Paddock Knoll."

And there I had a revelation,
The eyes of my imagination
Could venture past this humble home,
Build castles out of little stones.
And for all my great adventuring,
I found greatness in the simplest things.
So I've gladly laid my journey down,
My heart is settled in this town.
And forever keeps my peaceful soul,
The little stone cottage at Paddock Knoll.

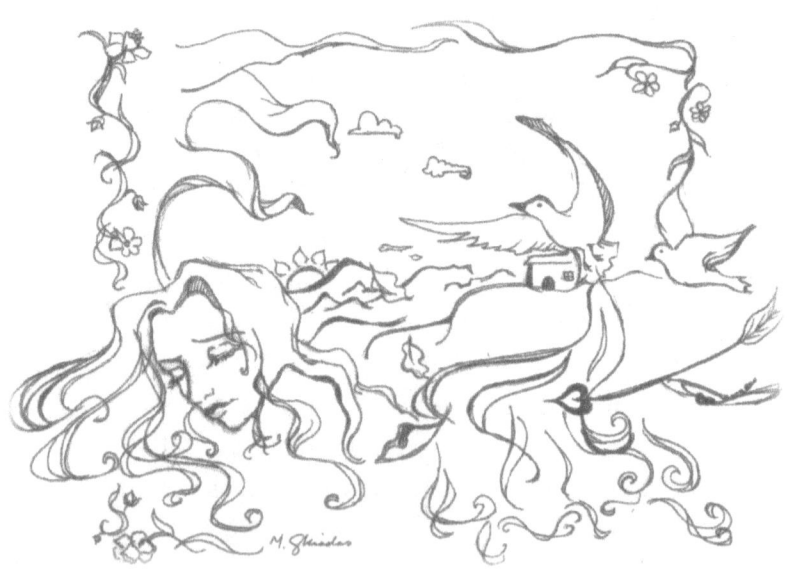

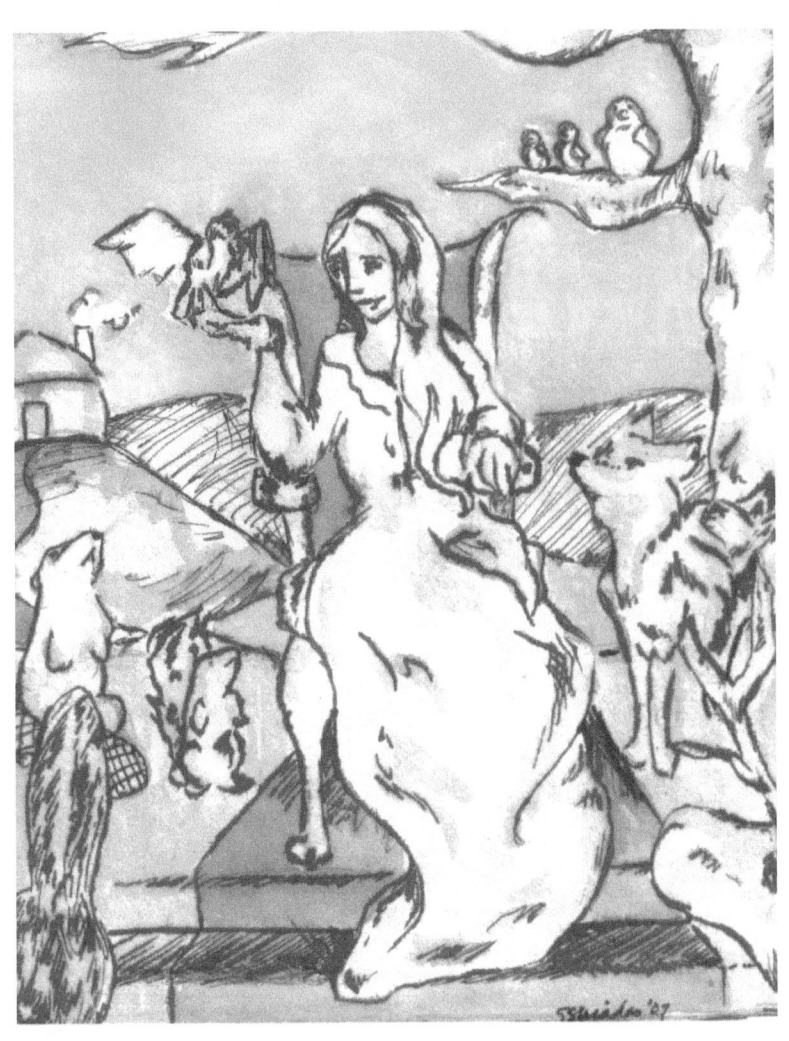

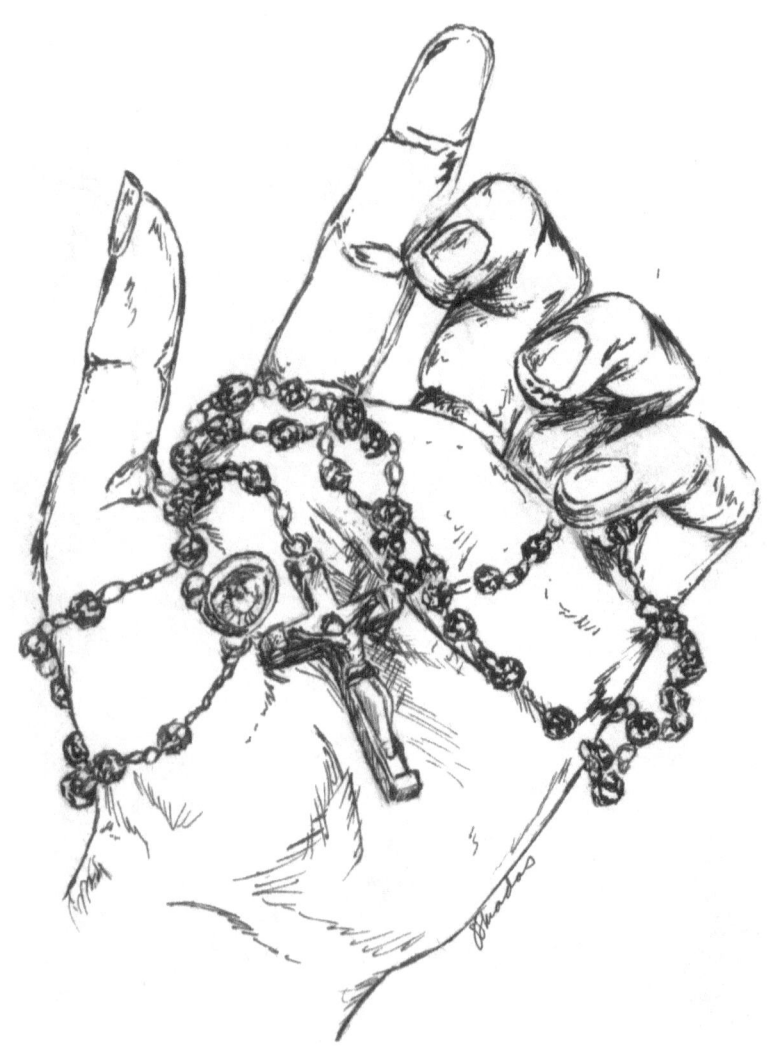

Saints Preserve Us
(Uncommon Prayer)

Uncommon among us are the good,
Unsought by us, misunderstood.
What of their motive, their holy care?
And yet they cause the world to stare.

They sparkle light from out their eyes.
They cause distrust amidst our lies
And torments of our bitter ways
Help to build them better days.

Their cares seem few, their interests deep.
While we lament they lose no sleep.
Among our peers they are so odd
But still we fail to see their god.

They say, "It is for you, our love,"
We turn away the light above.
They say, "It is for you, we die,"
We say, "We'd rather live the lie."

Though when we do expose our need
To prey upon their flesh and feed,
They turn to us with open sores
And say, "Someday we'll end your wars."

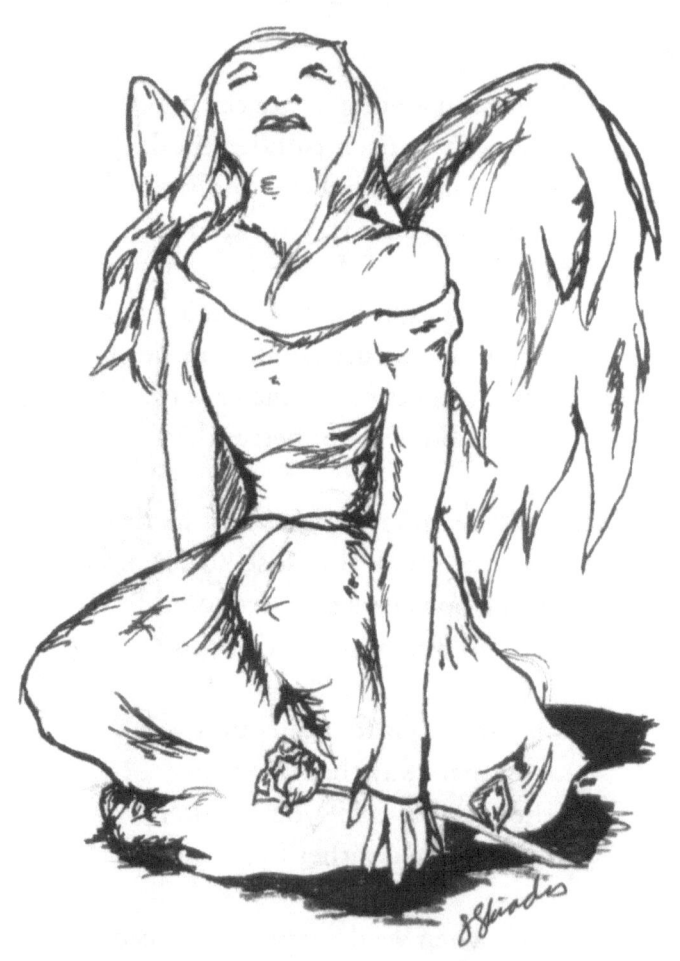

The Day Virginia's Angels Flew

Where were you that chilly morning,
Back in April, day was dawning,
When one of Blackburgh's broken sons
Raged through our heaven waving guns.

In Ambler Johnston two angels flew.
The first to fly of thirty two,
And our small heaven felt the change,
Became a hell of gun exchange.

For Norris Hall no warning blew
In time to save the thirty slew.
And madness took, before our eyes,
Friends and family from our lives.

Then thirty angels I saw fly
To join the others in the sky.
And I know they were angels true,
For those they saved when bullets flew.

The name, they say, for what occurred
Was headlined as "The Massacre"
But I will lend my memory to,
"The Day Virginia's Angel's Flew"

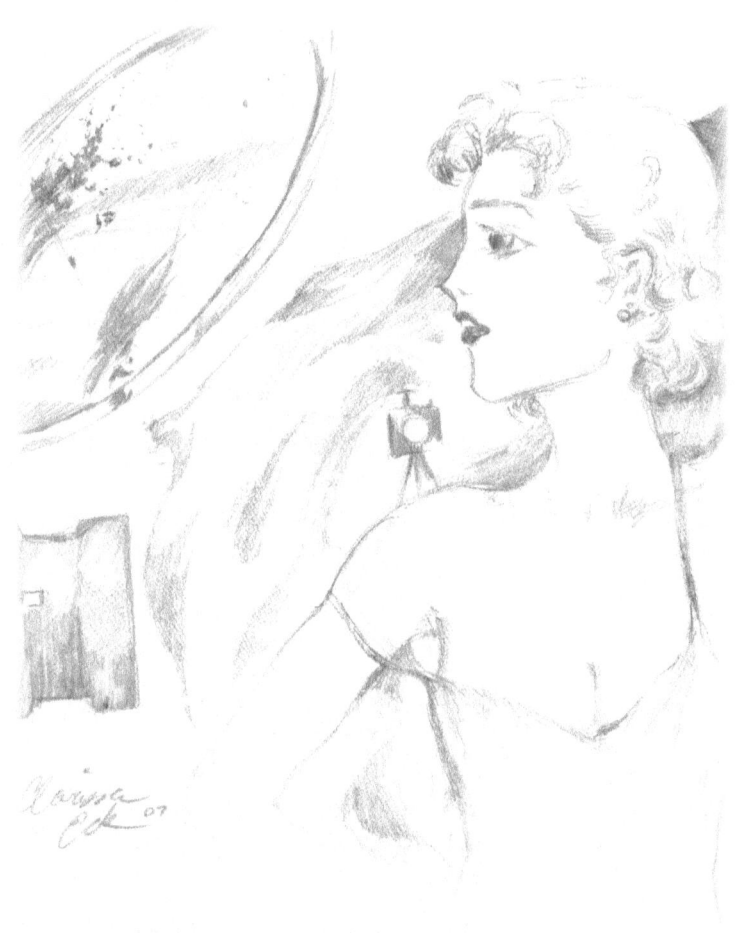

Legend and Myth

She looked like a doll
Dressed in satin and lace,
With the rest of her life
In a tiny suitcase.
And stepped off the bus
With such Hollywood grace,
That the world spun around her
And quickened its pace.

She was born in the moonlight,
A star studded child.
Not made for the life
Of the plain or the mild.
Cast in the flames
Of the famously styled.
A legend and myth,
She was nude in the wild.

She smiled and sighed
When the scripts told her so.
She could cry
At the drop of a leaf like a pro,
Then the tears in her eyes
Really started to flow,
And the colors all ran
From her colored rainbow.

She dared to imagine,
To be someone else,
Far away from the spotlights,
The news and the press,
And abandon the make up,
The hair and the dress,
And she dreamed that
It would be her greatest success.

In front of the masses
She poured out her charms,
And embraced the whole
Weight of the world in her arms,
But she woke in the morning
And damned the alarms.
And alone in her mirror
She died in her arms.

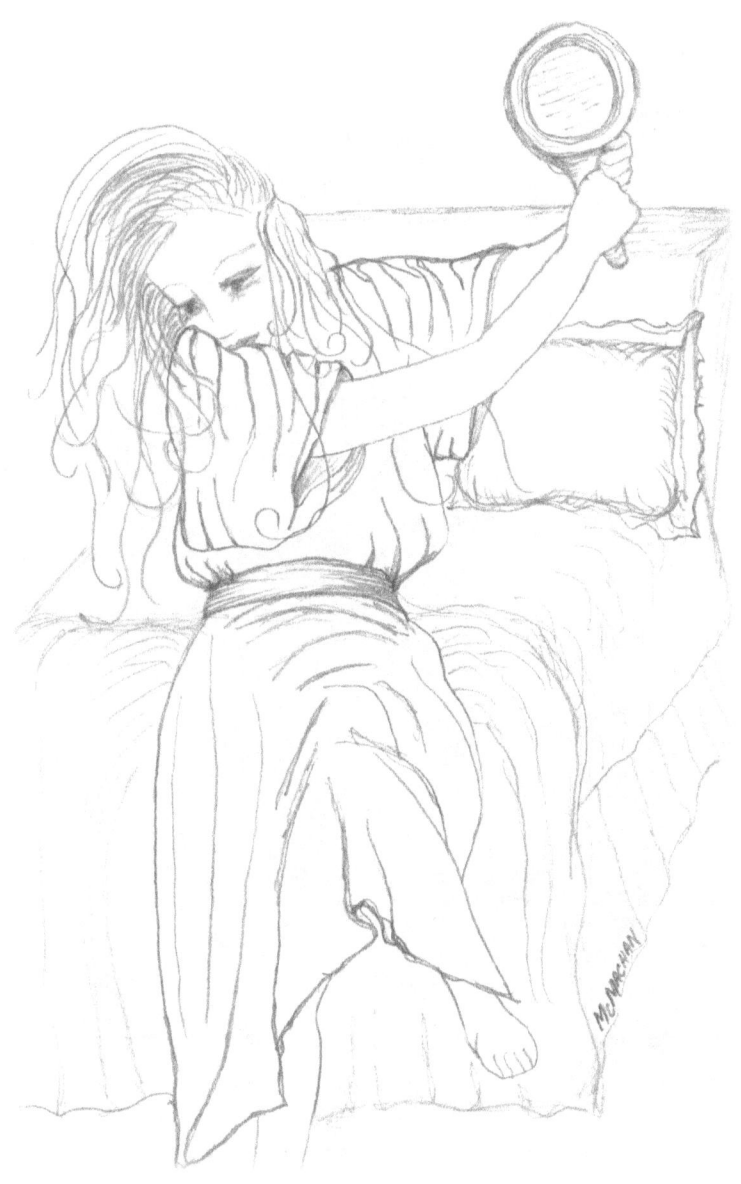

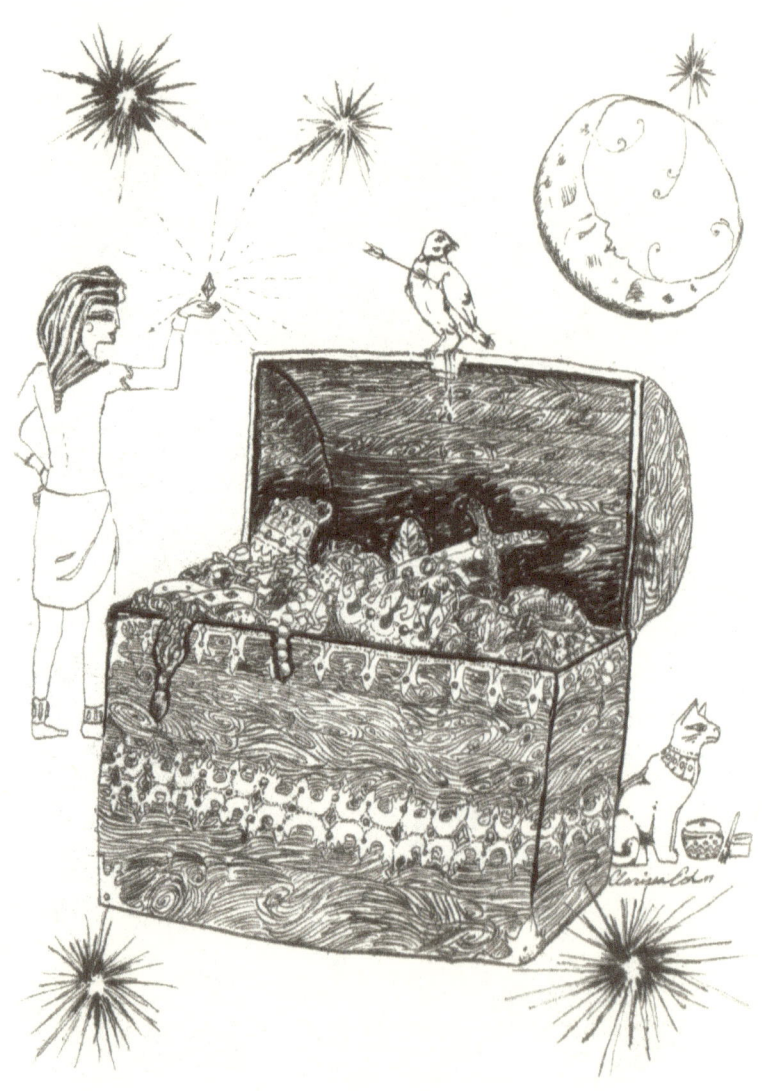

Hold a Grape The Sun has Kissed

Hold a Grape the sun has kissed,
it's Royal Purple Amethyst.
A Flash of red in a deep blue night
sparkles proudly Tanzanite
And sunny is the yellow sheen
of Lemon Quartz and Gold Citrine,
that pageant in march pizzazz
among the shades of rich Topaz.

Now, if a pigeon's blood should fall,
know that Ruby takes it all
and makes a deep red stone so fine
whose color looks like Bordeaux wine.
Cleopatra dressed in Peridot,
with it's green and other worldly glow.
And garnet wears all colors well
so do Tourmalines and gems Spinell

But the greenest field in all the world
has nothing on the Emerald,
that shows itself with kingly pride
while Tzars sport Chrome Diopside.
Challenge not it's royal might
if you come across Alexandrite
whose color changes all the time
though barren lays it's Russian mine.

Then toast champagne the Aussie way
with Diamonds in their final play.
And Pink and Chocolate colors too,
I'd have some now if I were you.
Constant is the bluish fire
that cools the Ceylon blue sapphire
whose mirror image is the sight
of the water rock called Iolite.

Kuntz found stones of pinkish hue,
then gave old Morgan pink ones too.
But Serenghetti didn't shrink
it's Rubies boast the hottest Pink.
Do not mistake a cubic pawn
for Zircon from the Age of Dawn,
with ancient secrets deep within
that measure earth's own origin.

While Jelly Opal's inner glory
tells us it's own water story.
And oceans wave and oceans curl
and throw out tiny spheres of Pearl.
But of all the gems that I've grown fond
Still, none compares to the Diamond
Whose brilliance is exquisite light
and fascinates with pure delight.

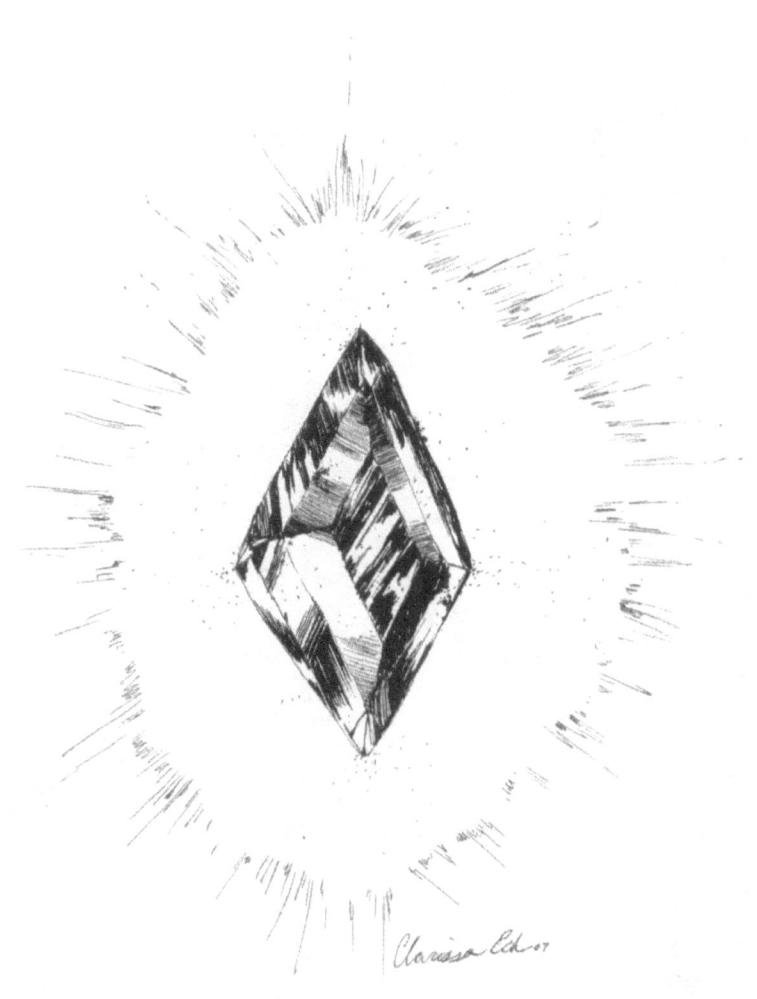

Clarissa Cole '07

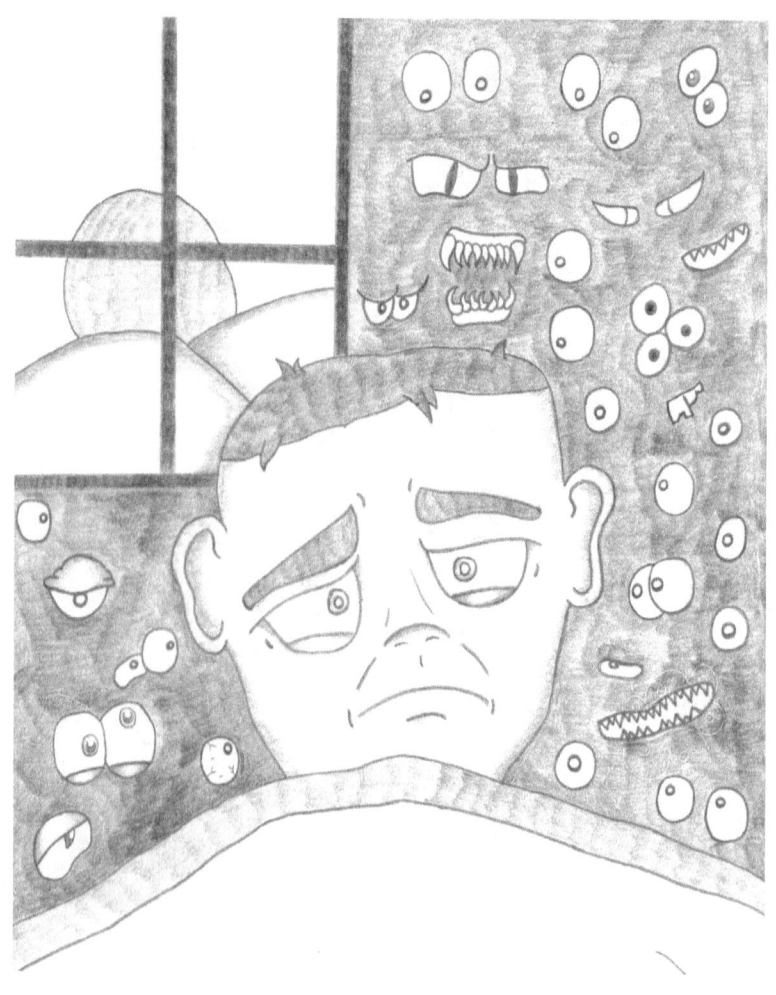

Light of Day

Vanishing, vanishing through the trees,
Days last light pulls Days last breeze
And rushes over west hills high
To refuge in the distant sky.

Then shadow monsters small and large
Become the black night's entourage
And creep beyond the forest clearing
Where I in my abode lay fearing,

And hold my blanket to my chin,
To stop the creatures' coming In.
I squeeze my eyes shut, hard and tight.
If I don't see them, they won't bite,

And plead with the Almighty Power
To spare me from the Devil's hour.
To take away the demons scary,
I pray to gentle Mother Mary.

And ask that Jesus do his best
To drive the shadows to the west,
And chase the cobalt night away,
To bring me back the light of day.

Make Love to Me

Make love to me, you are my home,
And never will I be alone.

Make love to me my spirit sighs,
I lie beneath your loving eyes.

Your mouth upon my lips, we kiss,
And ever, ever love like this.

Heat my skin with your desire,
Drown me in that loving fire,

And smolder on, together one,
Together hearts we have become,

So glad, my spirit lets you in,
Where bodies end and hearts begin.

The beating of our souls united,
Enter heaven uninvited.

And steal a place in paradise,
While bodies sway in earthly vice.

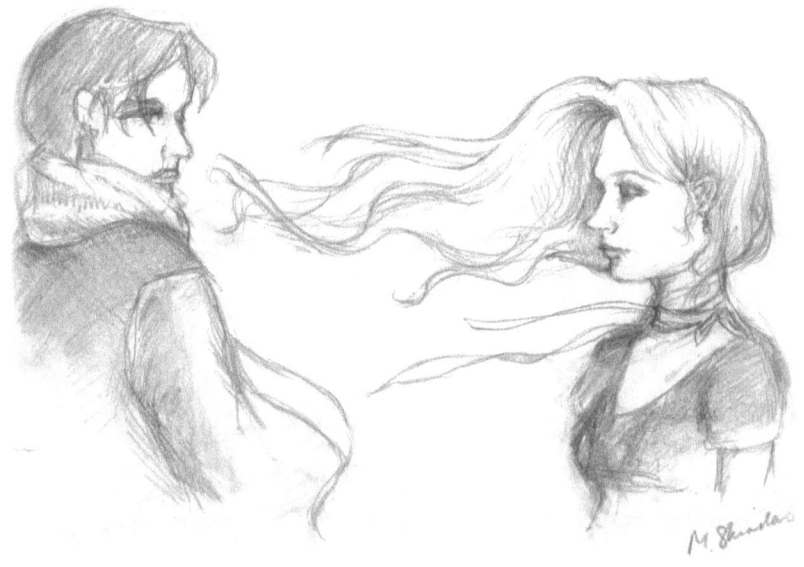

Forever hold me strong and fast,
And when our living days are past.

Embodied flesh all falls away,
Our bones but left in stark display,

We'll find ourselves in heavenly lands,
With spirit hearts and spirit hands.

Rejoice the union of our souls!
Rejoice! The spirit church bell tolls.

Then, make love to me in spirit form,
Make love to me, you are my home.

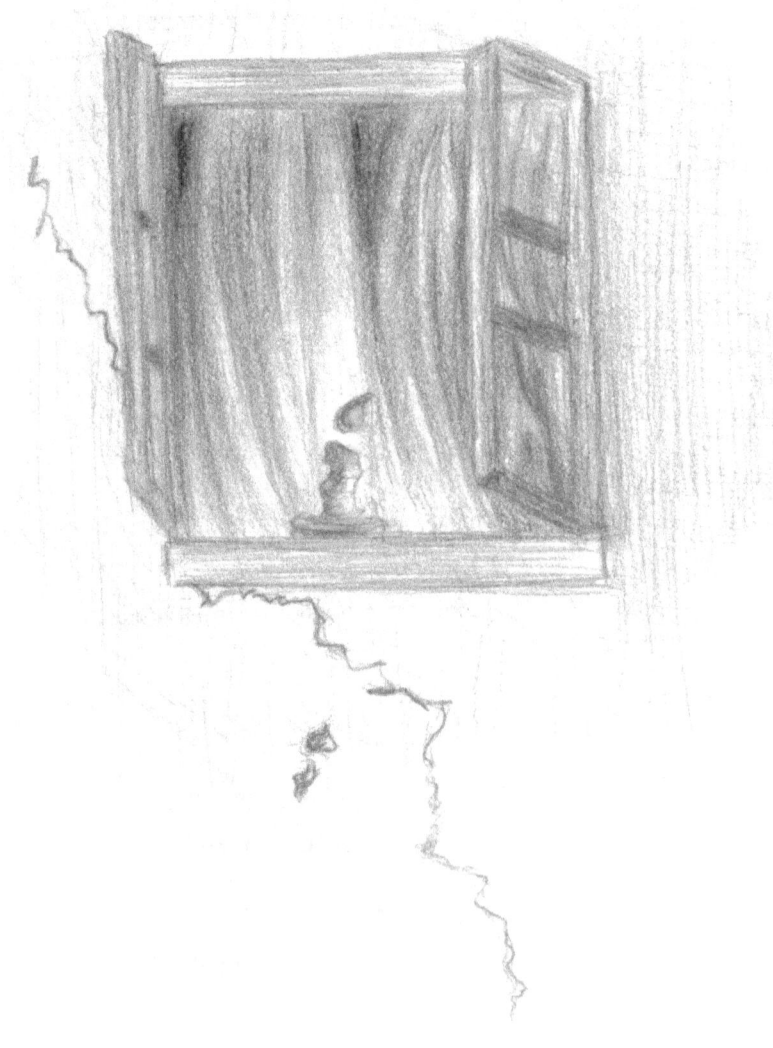

Light a Tapered Candle

Light a tapered candle,
And wait for me at night,
I will find my way to you,
By window's candlelight.

Whisper my name softly,
In the wind that I may hear,
The sweetness of its melody
Dancing in my ear.

Pour out your affections,
In all the winding streams,
And send them to the ocean,
Where I sail on ships of dreams.

Drop your pebbles on the trail,
A mark on every tree,
So I know that my journey,
Brings you near to me.

Keep the candle vigil,
So it lights my path with love,
And home my heart will fly to you,
On wings of Morning Doves.

www.ingramcontent.com/pod-product-compliance
Lightning Source LLC
Chambersburg PA
CBHW021922170526
45157CB00005B/2146